PLATFORM PAPERS

QUARTERLY ESSAYS ON
THE PERFORMING ARTS

||||||||||||||||||||||||||||||||||||||

No. 28
July 2011

CURRENCY HOUSE

PLATFORM PAPERS

Quarterly essays from Currency House Inc.

Editor: Dr John Golder, j.golder@unsw.edu.au

Currency House Inc. is a non-profit association and resource centre advocating the role of the performing arts in public life by research, debate and publication.

Postal address: PO Box 2270, Strawberry Hills, NSW 2012, Australia

Email: info@currencyhouse.org.au   Tel: (02) 9319 4953
Website: www.currencyhouse.org.au   Fax: (02) 9319 3649

Editorial Board: Katharine Brisbane AM, Michael Campbell, Dr John Golder, John McCallum, Martin Portus, Greig Tillotson

ISBN 978 0 9807982 5 8
ISSN 1449-583X
Typeset in 10.5 Arrus BT
Printed by Hyde Park Press, Richmond, SA
This edition of Platform Papers is supported by the Sidney Myer Fund, Neil Armfield, David Marr, Joanna Murray-Smith, Martin Portus, Alan Seymour and other individual donors and advisers. To them and to all our supporters Currency House extends sincere gratitude.

SIDNEY MYER FUND

Contents

AVAILABILITY *Platform Papers*, quarterly essays on the performing arts, is published every January, April, July and October and is available through bookshops or by subscription. For order form, see page 72.

LETTERS Currency House invites readers to submit letters of 400–1,000 words in response to the essays. Letters should be emailed to the Editor at info@currencyhouse.org.au or posted to Currency House at PO Box 2270, Strawberry Hills, NSW 2012, Australia. To be considered for the next issue, the letters must be received by 5 August.

CURRENCY HOUSE For membership details, see our website at: www.currencyhouse.org.au

The Fall and Rise of the VCA

The pulse in the arm

RICHARD MURPHET

*This Platform Paper is dedicated to
Lenton Parr, a visionary.*

The author

Richard Murphet has been working in theatre for three decades as writer, director, actor and teacher. He has written over ten plays, including *Quick Death, Slow Love, Dolores in the Department Store, The Inhabited Woman* (with Leisa Shelton) and *The Inhabited Man*. He has directed productions, in Melbourne, Sydney, Adelaide, Toronto, New York, Utrecht and Ghent, of work by writers as diverse as Sophocles, Euripides, Marlowe, Brecht, Fassbinder, Kroetz, Wertenbaker, Hibberd, Barker, Fornes, Pinter, Churchill, Ibsen, Shepard, Peeters and Breuer. His most recent work has been with the theatre ensemble Rear Windows, which he co-directs with Leisa Shelton: this has included *Dolores in the Department Store* (2000, 2001), *The Inhabited Woman* (2003) and *The Inhabited Man* (2008).

Richard is an honorary senior research fellow in Performing Arts at the Victorian College of the Arts and Music, University of Melbourne, where he was head of the Drama School from 2007 to 2009 and head of Postgraduate Studies in Drama from 1996 to 2006. His responsibilities at VCA have included training directors and performance makers, supervising Masters students, directing actors and training writers for theatre. In 1996 Richard received a Carrick Institute Award for Excellence in Tertiary Teaching. He was a member of the Australian Performing Group from 1975 to 1981, and artistic director of the Mill Theatre Company from 1985 to 1987. He is currently a PhD student at the University of Melbourne, researching rehearsal processes for the creation of new performance texts.

Acknowledgements

I am grateful to the following for kindly agreeing to be interviewed and allowing me to quote them or else to make use of their insights in this essay: Andrea Hull, Anthony Grigg, Brian Long, Elizabeth Presa, Ian McRae, Lynne Landy, Noel Turnbull, Lindy Davies, Noel Denton, Kristy Edmunds, Mark Pollard, Su Baker, Ros Walker and Sara Koller;

I should also like to thank Noel Denton, for the loan of the original 'Educational Specifications of the Victorian College of the Arts' document; Brian Long, for helping me access many of the key documents, reports and reviews connected to the amalgamation process; Jenny Kemp, for valuable editorial feedback; Katharine Brisbane, chair of Currency House, for inviting me to write this essay; and John Golder, for his detailed and sensitive editorial work on the manuscript.

Prologue

'The pulse in the arm less strong and stronger'

T. S. Eliot[1]

In his poem, 'Marina', T. S. Eliot chose to hold the wandering King Pericles at a point of transition, approaching the shore of his homeland after many years away. This moment at the brink is not one focused upon by Shakespeare, whose *Pericles* is an adventure story, filled with 'event'—with tragedy, hope, romance, loss, moral dilemma, treachery, accident, coincidence, travel and so on. In this stilled frame, as his boat nears the shore, Eliot's king holds the memories of these events within him still and as a result is no longer lost, but not yet found. In the face of the old familiar images of home, the smells and sounds that now fill his senses, all the memories of the struggle, violence, glory, contentment and ecstasy of his adventures '[a]re become unsubstantial'. Yet in truth it cannot be a return to home, since the intervening years with all their dramas have transformed Pericles; and the shifts and changes caused by the passage of time mean that his sense of anticipation is interwoven with a dread of not even recognizing the place when he arrives. Eliot begins the poem with a quotation from Seneca: 'What place is this, what kingdom, what part of the world?'[2] Yet at the very centre of the poem, a pulse beats, 'less strong and stronger'. Whether it is his own, or that of his daughter, it fades and surges like all pulses and signifies there is life ahead. It is the pulse of a life to which he will commit himself. Willing to exchange the life he has led 'for this life', he moves towards the future—'my daughter'—'awakened, lips parted', filled with 'hope', seeking to jettison the old ship he has built, with its 'rigging weak' and its 'canvas rotten', for 'new ships' in 'a world of time beyond me'.[3]

Introduction
A brief chronology of
the VCA[4]

1967   Art School established in State Gallery of Victoria
       (later National Gallery of Victoria).
1968   Lenton Parr appointed Head of National Gallery
       Art School.
1972   Victorian College of the Arts proclaimed, Parr ap-
       pointed Director. Established as an independent col-
       lege of higher learning within the Victorian Institute
       of Colleges, and located in buildings previously used
       as police barracks in St Kilda Rd.
1973   National Gallery Art School becomes foundation
       school of VCA.
1974   School of Music established, with John Hopkins as
       Founding Head.
1975   School of Drama established, with Peter Oyston as
       Founding Head.
1978   VCA Secondary School established.
1979   School of Dance established, with Anne Woolliams
       as Founding Head.
1985   Lionel Lawrence replaces Lenton Parr as Director
       of VCA.
1987   John Dawkins' Green Paper on higher education
       sets out radical shifts in organization of tertiary
       institutions.
1989   Alwynne Mackie replaces Lionel Lawrence as
       Director of VCA.
1991   VCA becomes an affiliate of University of
       Melbourne as a result of Dawkins' Green Paper.
1992   School of Film and TV established, with Jenny

Sabine as founding Head. Transferred from F&TV School at Swinburne Tech., established in 1966.

1995 Andrea Hull succeeds Alwynne Mackie as Director of VCA.

1998 Directors' Report to Council and Heads of Schools outlines major financial challenges. Three choices: 'we cut, we grow, we save'.

1998 VCA Curriculum Audit, chaired by Ken Robinson, recommends changes in areas of interdisciplinarity and contextual study. Leads to establishment of Centre for Ideas, with Nikos Papastergiardis as Founding Head.

1999 VCA Council adopts first VCA-wide business plan, 'Creating Our Future'.

2002 Wilin Centre for Indigenous Arts established, with Michelle Evans as Head.

2005 Howard Government introduces 'cluster' system of academic funding, the '[Brendan] Nelson Reform'.

2007 VCA becomes a Faculty of University of Melbourne; Glyn Davis is Vice-Chancellor.

2007 Introduction at the University of 'Growing Esteem', a new way of organizing degree structures, known as the 'Melbourne Model'.

2008 Centre for Cultural Partnerships established, with Sue Clark as Head.

2008 School of Performing Arts established by amalgamating Dance, Production and Drama, with Kristy Edmunds as Founding Head.

2009 VCA amalgamates with the University's Faculty of Music to become Faculty of VCA and Music.

2009 Sharman Pretty succeeds Andrea Hull as dean of the new Faculty.

2009-10 SaveVCA campaign gathers strong support and pressure is placed on the University.

2010   Review of VCA chaired by Ziggy Switkowski delivers report. Sharman Pretty resigns.

2010   VCA and Music separate into two distinct units in the Faculty, with VCA at Southbank and Music at Parkville. Su Baker is appointed Head of VCA.

On the world stage, the crisis that overtook the Victorian College of the Arts in 2009-10 was of minor importance. It did make the front page of the Melbourne broadsheet, the *Age*, and cooked away in its pages for several weeks. To be realistic, it was probably a time of slow news. There were certainly no earthquakes, or floods, or fires, or gangland slayings. Even the footy hadn't reached its yearly peak. Nevertheless, it was highly unusual, if not unprecedented, for the troubles of an arts-training college to hit the headlines, and there is no denying the public nerve that was tweaked by the campaign waged by SaveVCA, the city march in August 2009, and the heated discussions on radio, in the press and online. 'One of the things that really amazed' Ros Walker, of the SaveVCA organization,

> about the campaign was that we got 41,500 Facebook friends and we were getting huge hits. When a new article was posted, you'd get a thousand people reading [it] on the same day. Now that's people who are passionate about the arts.

The University of Melbourne underestimated the potential strength of this passion. But let's face it, we at the VCA did as well, we underestimated ourselves.

For the VCA itself, of course, the events of 2009–10 were not minor, but critical: they went to the very identity of the College and its possible future(s). But this would hardly seem justification for a Platform

Paper on the VCA, given the plight of other arts courses and schools throughout Australia that have either survived in compromised health, or folded or been seriously emasculated, over the past few years. The immediate issues were political, financial and bureaucratic. However, sitting behind these factors was an extraordinary confluence of strands that make the 'VCA event' a fascinating case study of the place of arts training in a contemporary context. The strands that were interwoven throughout this period, and that still remain as pressing issues, were artistic, educational, organizational, financial, political, social and philosophical. They have to do with the particular history of the VCA, the specific timing of the crisis, and the parties involved. But they also raise questions that go way beyond the VCA case alone; in fact, it is clear that the kind of struggle the VCA faced and continues to face is going on in many higher-education institutions around the world.[5] In arts-training institutes, the questions are to do with pedagogic relevance, a sense of direction forward, training processes, the nature of artistic practice, the possibility of a distinctive identity within a large corporate structure, the ethics of takeover behaviour, and so forth.

I should say at the outset that this essay is not research of solely historical interest. The immediate crisis may have been averted, but the factors that gave rise to it are still unresolved. As I write, the VCA is engaged in an ongoing process of defining its modus operandi into the future. I have had to choose an arbitrary cut-off point for this survey—which is the start of 2011, the time of writing—but things continue to change daily, which is surely the sign of a pulse still beating; of an organization vitally alive, unwilling to settle into old patterns, knowing like Pericles that the future has to be made, and, in order to be made, has to be committed to. If anything, the period of crisis brought this vitality to the fore: both staff and students committed themselves to a wider political battle than the normal problems of creating one's work of art. It is my hope that, in this time of lively debate, the present essay will be an active element in the ongoing construction, rather than simply a record of events that have already 'become unsubstantial'.

In yet another disclaimer, I abjure any degree of objectivity in my overview. I have been on the VCA staff on and off for 30 years, training actors, directors, writers and animateurs in the School of Drama/Theatre/ Performing Arts. I resigned at the end of 2009, but remain as an honorary research fellow at the time of writing. This gives me some distance from which to look at the past few years; I no longer depend upon the College or the University for a living. But at the time of the 'VCA crisis' I was in the thick of it as Head of the Theatre School, attempting to deal with the unfolding events, while keeping the courses going. The fact that my experience has been in theatre training means, pre- dictably, that I shall be drawing the larger proportion of my material from that School. I have, however, tried to cover the wider range of arts taught at the VCA, and I hope that the arguments specific to Theatre shed light on the other areas. I have interviewed many people who have been involved in different aspects of the events as they happened, so I will be merging my own reading of the symptoms and ramifications of the unfolding situation with the considered opinions of others.

Finally, I have to say that I believe that the estab- lishment of the VCA in 1972 as a multi-arts training institute was an act of visionary prescience unequalled in the arena of tertiary arts training in Australia; and that in its maturation it has developed features of a model of high-quality training in specific arts disciplines within the larger context of a community of artists able to research outside the boundaries of their own art form. As we shall see, the potential of this model has not yet been fully realized at the VCA. But it is significant that when plans were being developed to set up multi-arts training institutes in Singapore, Hong Kong and Seoul, those concerned visited the VCA, seeking advice and inspiration from one of the few such academies in the world—and the only one positioned in the heart of the arts precinct of its city. I mention all this, not as a marketing push for the College, but as a measure of what was at stake in the battle that ensued between 2008 and 2010 for the right to determine the particular nature and shape that its future should take.

The culture at the VCA is quite particular and difficult to explain to those who have not experienced it. It is not in any way superior to the culture existing in other arts-training institutes, but it is different. It is symbolized by the logo designed at the outset by the founder, Lenton Parr, who described it as

> a form of pentagram; a traditional symbol for the five senses. It thus refers to the various modes of perception and, by implication, to their aesthetic functions in the various arts. The five principal curves comprising the figure are in reality a single continuously interweaving band and this alludes to the unity and interrelation of the several arts the College seeks to promote.[6]

The sheer diversity of artists at work and art practice on show on the campus has its effect, even if all the students spend most of their time on training in their chosen field. It was that culture that was on display in the SaveVCA campaign, when students from across the campus combined their artistic talents and spoke out with one voice. The immediate terms of the battle were, as I have said, to do with finance, bureaucracy and politics. However, so that we don't lose sight of the prime artistic and educational focus of the VCA, I want to begin by looking at the issues of art and education, which have informed debate at the College since it began. If one listens beneath the surface cacophony of the recent battle, these issues sound as key motifs. They are, moreover, issues of art and art training that would seem to me to have relevance far beyond this specific struggle of this specific institution.

1

Art, education and training

The Victorian College of the Arts was conceived, planned and established in the early 1970s, and the 'educational specifications' that constituted its philosophical and organizational charter were set down in 1974. These years were in the middle of one of the phases of the shifts and changes in arts-training philosophy that took place during the twentieth century. Simon Shepherd traces the concept of training itself from the mid-sixteenth-century training of soldiers as a cohesive force 'to ensure they obeyed orders and kept discipline'.[7] In the eighteenth century, as an alternative to the standard master-apprentice or generational handing down of medical knowledge, a specific training developed for surgeons 'based on practice and empirical evidence, the demonstration of dissection'. The twentieth century began with a vision for training that posited experimentation in addition to craft expertise as one of the goals of training. In their 1904 proposal for an actors' training school to be attached to the new National Theatre in England, William Archer and Harley Granville Barker envisioned that the school would not only provide the company with actors, but also keep 'the theatre's practices in touch with the modern world'. The training program was not there just to teach what already existed, but as 'an agent of modernity [...], a new sort of approach both to art and to work'.[8]

All the features of training mentioned above have direct relevance to the specific nature of the pedagogy at the VCA and at similar arts-training institutes: the transmission of skill and technique, the creation of coherent group entities, the sense of existing outside traditional structures, and training based upon immersive practice. The twin prongs—providing artists for the existing profession, and acting as 'an agent of modernity'—have been defining forces, though often at odds, at the VCA from its outset.

In the early decades of the twentieth century, theatre schools established these philosophies of training as distinct objectives: on the one hand, by a training in the Russian realist school identified with Stanislavski,

which prepared an actor for a deep, realistic representation of the dramatic theatre as it existed, and, on
the other, by a non-naturalistic, 'abstracted, practice,
not bound by the needs of realist representation',
connected to the avant-garde abstract forms being
developed in the other arts. This latter approach laid
emphasis on discovering means of vocal and physical
expression that accessed private, inner impulses, at the
same time as finding ways in which group action could
re-connect us to our communal, spiritual, 'liturgical'
roots—an evocation, it was thought, of a tribal past.
This training, with its pretensions towards a radical
experimentation, continued the track towards the new
and unusual, as distinct from what already existed.
But after World War II the 'effete' tendencies of
avant-garde abstraction were thought to be connected
solely to the concerns of a privileged class, and discon-
nected from the daily life of the working masses. Joan
Littlewood, the founder of the Theatre Workshop in
the 1950s, saw London's Royal Academy of Dramatic
Art as teaching only 'poise, propriety and "tricks of the
trade"'. In its place, there developed the 'commitment
to a more inclusive, democratized, theatre practice'
and training, and from there it was not a large step
to the radical reaction against training itself that developed throughout the 1960s.[9] Shepherd points out
that the rejection was not only of theatre training, but
of any kind of institutionalized education. The vision
propounded in books such as Ivan Illich's *Deschooling
Society* was not of a training process, which would
impose an ethics, an aesthetic and a set of behaviours,
but of an 'untraining' process that could liberate the
individual from social constraints and limitations in
order to release their artistic impulses.[10] If anyone is

an artist, if anyone can act, then the aim should be to free 'the artist within' and to encourage the open expression of each individual's creativity—instead of training, play; instead of structured drama, improvisation; instead of mass liturgies, group happenings.

The opening lines of the College's educational philosophy, as enunciated in 1974, set the parameters quite clearly:

> It is in the nature of the creative and interpretive arts that they achieve excellence through the cultivation of individual talent. Much can be transmitted by teaching what is customary practice and theory. Much depends upon a foundation of traditional skills and knowledge. Experience can be shared, faults corrected, goals set and so on, but in the long run an artist's stock-in-trade is his individuality, his personal vision and style. It follows that every student is capable of distinction only to the extent that his unique capabilities are fostered.[11]

The teaching process had to be shaped in such a way as to encourage students to attain this goal of artistic liberation:

> So far as possible then, an impersonal, set syllabus is avoided in favour of an extemporized and exploratory collaboration between the teacher and each student or ensemble of students. Goals are not so much pre-determined as invented in the process.

In the end, the vocation for which students were to be prepared was not only a career path in the profession, 'but also the special significance of a "calling", the life-long pursuit of self-realization by creative work'.[12]

We have to remember that the man who formulated the expression of this philosophy was Lenton Parr, who at the time was Head not only of the VCA, but also of the VCA School of Art. Indeed, when he first moved to establish an independent multi-arts campus, he had been Head of the National Gallery Arts School. Visual Art had a strong historical tradition from early in the twentieth century for claiming the uniquely individual; and likewise 'the relatively unstructured approach to art teaching' practised at the VCA 'derives from the Fine Art Academies of Europe, whose methods were determined by the real vocational needs of artists'. The Educational Specifications were clear about these 'real vocational needs': 'Visual fine artists are essentially people who generate ideas and images, and communicate them to others by display.'[13]

The Schools of Music and Dance, emerging as they did from training programs more classical in their focus, and depending as they did upon technique ingrained in students by years of secondary-school training, had pedagogies less concerned with the individuality of the practitioner. Traditionally both are ensemble art forms, their artists being prepared for work in the orchestras and dance companies that for the most part interpret the classical repertoire. In the case of Music, for instance, the 1974 Specifications stated that

> the principal involvement of the student with the School [would be] in ensemble and orchestral situations. Selection of students is in part directed towards establishing several such performing groups. This provides the means for students to become accomplished orchestral players, to participate in group learning, and to acquire an extensive repertoire of musical compositions.[14]

As Mark Pollard, composer and long-time teacher at the Music School, put it: 'The School was set up as a specialist orchestral-training institute to feed the Melbourne Symphony Orchestra and orchestras nationally.' Pollard currently heads up the New Music stream in the Department of the Victorian College of the Arts, within the wider Faculty of VCA and Music. The New Music stream is now separate from the bulk of instrumental-music training, which is located on the Parkville campus rather than down at VCA in Southbank. This split in Music training is one of the results of the recent restructuring of the VCA at the University of Melbourne, and, as Pollard admits, 'If you look at it from the outside, it's crazy'. However, as he goes on to explain, in a sense the split allows the VCA in Southbank to focus firmly on the creation of original contemporary music, and Music at Parkville on the interpretation and composition of 'art' music—making a student's choice simple: 'what already exists' or 'an agent of modernity'. In Pollard's words:

> One of the problems for amalgamation was that there were too many competing aesthetics and modes of teaching and associated cultural heritage for each location. In that sense, this model cleans it up for those involved and for those making a choice about each institution.

Over the past few decades the curriculum focus of the Dance School has shifted towards more contemporary dance forms, and consequently to encouraging the creation of original solo and small-group work. But the School originally arose from the ashes of the classically focused Ballet Victoria School, and moreover, the Foundation Head of Dance, Anne Woolliams, arrived from the Australian Ballet. In the early years, the School was seen as a direct competitor to the Australian Ballet School. More recently, however, it has offered contemporary alternatives to the classical, ensemble focus of the ABS.

The School of Drama has had a completely different trajectory. It is the only one of the foundation schools at the VCA not to emerge from a pre-existing training academy. In some sense it has swung in focus between classical training and new approaches, or a healthy mix of the two, depending upon who has been at the helm. It began with a carte blanche and a vision that paralleled not the traditional British or European models, but the radical theatre scene then existing in Melbourne. This scene was dominated at the time by the Australian Performing Group, which was set up at La Mama Theatre in Carlton in the late 1960s, moved in the early 1970s around the corner to an old pram factory site, and was finally closed at the end of the decade. Both organizationally and theatrically, the APG exhibited an amazing confluence of the trends of the period: a commitment to political activism and to texts that provided a political analysis of current and historical events, a prioritizing of new Australian work that dealt with aspects of the national identity, a democratization of work practices, and a wariness of the semblance of 'trained' acting. The APG was a cultural phenomenon of the 1970s Melbourne and it is not surprising that in its infancy the Drama School at the VCA drew staff from members of the APG, nor that its aesthetic philosophy paralleled that operative at the Pram.

I am choosing my words carefully here, since Peter Oyston, the Foundation Head of Drama, was not directly connected to the APG, nor was he consciously drawing inspiration from it. Oyston had lived and worked in theatre in the United Kingdom for several years at the time he successfully applied for the job of heading up a new Drama School in 1975. It was in England that he had come across the community-theatre movement. On the other hand, his vision for the School was certainly built on a radical view similar to that of the APG, namely that theatre could be a central player in Australian society. He envisioned the School not as another NIDA, with a training pedagogy in the mould of the traditional British academy, but as an intensive preparation for the formation of a series of new companies, making new work, fresh in style and purpose, and relevant to the community in which they operated. The curriculum emphasized play, creativity, group dynamics, dramaturgy and a bold performance style. The work created was either socially committed original performance, or self-consciously local adaptations of pre-existing texts. Graduates formed graduating companies, working in the country regions of Victoria, or in the suburbs of Melbourne, creating work for their local community. Most of these companies were highly successful and formed the backbone of the vibrant community-theatre movement that flourished in Victoria in the '70s and '80s.

My summary of all this is by default reductive, but essentially this was a pedagogy mid-century style, liberating itself from the shackles of tradition. In its extremity it hit up against two key obstacles, one of which related to the planned philosophy for the School, while the other emerged from the socio-political backlash to the 'liberated' '60s, the effect of which we are still feeling/suffering.

Although they were careful not to 'pre-empt the educational philosophy of the future Dean', the Educational Specifications were fairly clear on the kind of training expected in the Drama School: 'Fundamental to the professional studies will be a basis of classical acting technique supported by thorough voice and movement training.'[15] If this was what was expected in 1974, it was not exactly evident in the program that Oyston set up.[16] There was no doubting that his vision saw the School as an agent of modernity, but it was believed to have failed in the preparation of students for performing in the existing profession. According to Noel Denton, who was General Manager of the VCA at the time, John Sumner, Artistic Director of the Melbourne Theatre Company and strongly supportive of the establishment of the School, was known to be dismayed at the direction the course had taken. But the clash really manifested itself at the level of educational philosophy rather than pragmatics. When Lindy Davies was appointed Head of Acting, she brought personal experience of a form of training that had helped shape a major strand in the history of actor training in the latter part of the twentieth century:

> I was originally invited to go there [to the VCA] when I was in Paris in the middle of the [Peter] Brook experience; the amazing thing of making work with classicism at the basis of it.

Herein lay the heart of the difference of opinion:

> My problem at that time was a philosophical difference, in that I believed both that the classics were important and that to make new work you had to be profoundly skilled.

Davies left before the clash of directions had been fully worked through, but the shift was in progress, and the Acting course was split into two streams, which encapsulated the two philosophies of training. When

Oyston resigned in 1984, his replacement, Roger Hodgman (and later his successor David Latham), changed the curriculum over to a training that would prepare students not for making new work in the regions of country Victoria, but for work in companies such as the MTC, of which Hodgman took over the artistic directorship when John Sumner resigned in the late 1980s. When Lindy Davies returned in 1995 to become Head of Drama, she built her curriculum from the policies she had proposed in her 'Autonomous Actor' document, originally written in the early '70s, 'in the spirit of Lenton Parr's [Educational Specifications] document'.[17] It was a curriculum in which a thorough training in skill techniques formed a strong base for an actor able ideally to work with autonomy both in the interpretation of the canon of dramatic theatre texts and in the creation of contemporary theatre.

The wider developments in the training of artists that appeared post-1970s are intimated in the brief coverage of the acting curriculum above. Simon Shepherd marks one of the shifts from the mid-1980s, and the fight-back by late capitalism against the liberalism of the previous decade:

> But while the artists and thinkers had attacked training for its complicity with capitalist values, in the mid-1980s capitalism's government continued this assault by other means. [...] In its place came a society of amateurism in high places, advancement on the basis of ruthlessness and greed, and an expansion of service industries: a culture where the only valued skills were 'interpersonal' ones, charm without respect.[18]

In Australia, this increase in governmental control is now associated with the release in 1987 of the Dawkins

Green Paper on Higher Education. In fact, this paper was one of a number of reports brought out by the Ministry for Education and Training over the years 1987-89, all of which sought from different angles to re-structure tertiary and workshop education and training in the light of 'the major economic challenges now facing Australia'. The focus was not upon the specifics of training, but upon its 'arrangement'. The demands to be met were no longer to do with questions of 'human fulfillment', but with 'the structure of the economy' and 'Australia's international competitiveness':

> The adjustments required in the structure of the economy, and improvements in Australia's international competitiveness, will make heavy demands on our human resources and labour force skills. Our skills formation and training arrangements are not yet adequate to meet those demands.[19]

The restructuring was indicative, as Judith Bessant notes, of a conception of education and training as part of the market economy:

> Permeating the public sector and particularly the education system, this 'new' mindset was characterized by the increased prevalence and use of economic paradigms, the indiscriminate application of market models and values, a commitment to notions of user-pays systems and the widespread application of entrepreneurial language and practices. Paralleling this trend was a widespread backlash against what came to be generally seen as the social and fiscal irresponsibility of in [sic] the progressives said to have held the reigns [sic] until the mid 1970s.[20]

The Dawkins Green Paper prompted the changes that culminated with Brendan Nelson's 'cluster' reform in 2003 (of which more presently). The outcome, for the

VCA, was the initial stage of its interconnection with the University of Melbourne. There is little doubt that the preference on the part of the bureaucrats in charge of implementing the Green Paper was for an immediate full amalgamation of the two institutions. However, the agreement that emerged was what Andrea Hull has called 'an elegant affiliation':

> My take on the affiliation was that it was the most fantastic example of genuine creative thinking. It was David Pennington's genius. He was the University of Melbourne Vice-Chancellor and hated what Dawkins was doing to higher education. He didn't think that amalgamation was the answer for the VCA. So between him and the chair of the VCA Council they worked out an elegant way to comply with the Dawkins model, with the narrowest of margins in directions, but at the same time managing to preserve the special features of its charter. We never gave up our legislative base, we had our own Act, the VCA Council was responsible for plant, staff and operations, but students of the VCA were students of the University, doing a curriculum that had been approved through university systems. The elegance was in working out how close to the margins you could go, to preserve the features and allow the VCA to receive its funding through the 'postbox' of the University.

The hands-off policy of affiliation preserved for the VCA a large degree of independence, while assuring it a 'home' within a powerful and renowned institution. It is this 'elegant' status that has been removed in the latest policy change of amalgamation, and in the opinion of most of those disturbed by the merger a return to the affiliate status, were it possible, would be the best of all solutions.

There is a belief, nevertheless, that, however elegant the 1980s managerial shift, with it began a noticeable movement of power away from the separate units of the schools of training and into the hands of a centralized bureaucracy. For some, like Andrea Hull and VCA manager Anthony Grigg, this was both inevitable as the College grew in size and complexity, and necessary in order to give real shape to the cohesive multi-arts campus that Lenton Parr had envisioned. Said Andrea Hull:

> I was staggered in 1995, when I took over, that the staff [of the various Schools] did not know each other. They […] had no way of interacting. I found the economies of scale shocking; that each School was running everything independently, with separate administrations, separate publicity policies, separate fund-raising strategies. […] There was no sense of cohesion, no overall shape to what a VCA was. But Lenton's vision was really cohesive.

For Lindy Davies, whose bailiwick was the actual training of the artists, this bureaucratic shift deprived the training programs of power and undermined their effectiveness:

> When I arrived in 1995, no matter how beaten down things were, there was still the fact that the funding and power lay with the schools. We had been a community of artists in which people disagreed, argued, had passionate fights, but we were fiercely interdependent because we had something of shared value. This changed after '99 and the bureaucrats took over. During the '80s, when all the artists were forced to go underground, the bureaucrats weren't underground; they were forming a culture that didn't need us. My perspective was always that if you give artists a problem, they can solve it because they can bring their originality to it.

In fact, and despite the alteration in power dynamics, during the two decades from 'Dawkins' to amalgamation, the VCA did find a way of operating successfully both administratively and educationally, somehow balancing the demands of the Schools with the needs of the complex institution it had become. This was due to an overall maturation of the culture of the VCA, under Andrea Hull's strong leadership, intelligent administrators at School level, and a consolidation of effective teaching staff in each area. They combined fine skills in training with ongoing work as independent artists, and this gave them a direct connection to the art form for which they were preparing their students. With the aid of a newly established marketing team, the VCA brand spread nationally and internationally. The campus was active, student work appeared everywhere, graduates gained national and international recognition, and there was a growing sense of ownership not only of the specific Schools, but also of the College as a whole. In particular, and notwithstanding the tensions over authority, there was a commitment to the mission of the VCA on the part of the central administrative staff themselves, many of whom had already been with the College for several years. I think that this was a key factor, and stands in stark contrast to the disconnect between administration and the core business of artist training that has grown since the amalgamation of the VCA and the University.

Nevertheless, the administrative balancing act was one that avoided really effective action to balance the finances. From the point of view of Sara Koller, a School administrator, the fault lay in the head-in-the-sand attitude of the heads of schools:

None of the heads of schools have been business people at any level. They don't really know how to read a budget—are not really interested in it. And yet they were the ones with all the power. Unless they sought advice or had a few clues, this area got ignored.

Combining art and business is not easy, as those artistic directors and company managers faced with the constant challenge of grant submissions are only too aware. The issue is not to do with the undeniable necessity for a financial sense of responsibility, but of where one lays down the lines of priority. The 1980s shifted the lines to such a degree that art making and art training have either shuddered or gone under with the strain, or have had to redefine their core principles:

It gets back to what is it that a society values. The '80s caused a revolution in the world—the values were greed and outcome. So artists essentially were devalued and dismissed, giving over to the rise of the celebrity. So the only way that any significant funding can actually happen is if society takes on board again that the arts are fundamentally important to it.

Or, to quote Anthony Grigg, a bureaucrat horrified by the shift in priorities:

We get back to choice between the humanist approach to education as opposed to the utilitarian approach, an approach which causes us now to talk about 'training', instead of 'education'.

This positioning of art in the marketplace of late capitalism has had a deep effect upon our understanding of 'art' itself. Gary Willis has recently developed a polemic for the restitution of '[t]he imaginative realm of the true arts [that] calls upon deep intuitive instincts to precipitate conceptual gestalt'. He sees this realm as under threat from the reconceptualisation of art as a 'completely instrumentalised' production:

> While public, corporate and private collecting habits are being reconfigured to support public initiatives, art produced outside these highly politicized networks is abandoned to survive the marketplace. Outside of these networks, art competes for market-share with furniture, fashion and the entertainment industries, where the promotional agencies have appropriated art strategies to market commodity culture and vice-versa. [...] Ethics have displaced aesthetics, the collaborative network has displaced the independent initiative and art is secondary to the academic imperative, which sustains art's professional classes, 'publish or perish'.

Willis's argument is a conservative one, in the true meaning of that word: it seeks to conserve the traditional philosophical concept of 'high' art in the face of contemporary moves to bring art to a wider demographic: 'The origin of art is profound knowledge and must not be trivialized by the reduction of art to the diversions of leisure.'[21]

There are, of course, many rejoinders to such a position. In fact, much of the heat in the arguments around postmodernism has been generated by exactly this blurring of the distinction between high and low art forms ['eternal truths' versus 'fashion']. In the pages of his much wider argument, Willis occasionally draws out some of the implications for arts training:

> This irrelevance of art's history represents the crisis for 'art' education. What does the study of art have to offer that is not already on offer in the study of other disciplines; new media, visual culture, creative

industry, fashion, film or industrial design?'

For Su Baker, Head of the School of Art (2000–10), and now Director of the VCA, the issues raised by Willis have to do not so much with the philosophy of art as with methods of doing it and teaching it.

> There is a whole return to the aesthetic in the criticism in the field. This is not a return to basics and to the canon, but an argument that embodied practice and material practice need to have a value.

That is, in contrast to a broader study of art, which is, in Willis' words, 'being absorbed into broader cross-disciplinary programs, which represent issues common to all contemporary culture',[22] Baker is underscoring the immersive training in embodied and material art practised at the VCA from the outset.

For Mark Pollard, busy setting the agenda for the contemporary music stream at the VCA, the issue is already decided:

> If you look at iTunes, you would find fifty different categories of music or more. [...] Those who are in jobs are very quick to take the moral high ground when it comes to art making, all the while knowing that you are basically condemning your graduates to unemployment. That has always bothered me and to me this was the chance to drag commercial music somewhere else. It's a matter of saying 'OK, this is the space between, everyone wants it, it's not going anywhere, let's just grab it and take it somewhere while there's a window to do it.' It would have been easier to stay in the Conservatory, but the heart feels good—and that's the VCA difference.

For Lindy Davies, on the other hand, '[t]he decade of the '80s, with its focus upon product, outcome, economic imperatives, accountability wiped out the original voice and saw the evolution of a philosophy of postmodernism—the bottom line of which is that you don't value things'.

In the sphere of training, this threat to the 'original voice' threatened not only the student artist, but also the teacher whose power as a mentor was seriously undermined by the spread of relativity into the domain of culture and education. The question of where the power lies, who exercises authority, has become debatable, as has the very concept of communicating value-systems in a training process. Modernism saw a struggle to locate some ineluctable truths, not by following science's path of deductive reasoning, but by highlighting the processes of intuition and dialogue. The radical rethinking in which the postmodernists engaged undermined any faith in the worth of such a search. In many ways this is a positive step, unseating authorities that have simply assumed the seats of power. But the effect, at least during the transition stage, is also unsettling; and the breakdown of the teacher-mentor role throws open the question of what the nature of a training process can be.

This sense of loss of direction was reinforced by shifts at the micro level of administration. Issues such as staff/student-number ratios, the amount of attention paid to assessment, the centralization of timetabling, and the rationalization of space usage have only served to reduce the scope for autonomous decision-making on the part of staff and students involved in the day-to-day training process. This loss of power, however logical in bureaucratic terms, can only cause extreme alarm when, as has happened, the power lands in the hands of people who have little interest in that absolutely essential, but inexplicable, 'implicit' quality that is at the heart of all great teaching. By 'implicit' teaching I mean those aspects of learning that happen outside any curriculum plan, and are to do with how an artist with experience passes on the subtleties of art practice that go beyond sheer technique. However well-organized courses might be, it is the quality of implicit teaching that prepares the ground for deep learning to take place. But it takes time and confidence and a special bond between artist and mentor. It cannot be programmed, but it can be choked by insensitive programming decisions.

In the face of this potential crisis of faith at the heart of training, two paths presented themselves as ways forward. One was to return with rejuvenated energy to a belief in the deep truths of art, and to revivify and in a sense 'personalize' the skills necessary for an artist to achieve these. In theatre, during the 1970s, '80s and '90s, a range of influential practitioners, such as Jerzy Grotowski, Peter Brook, Eugenio Barba and Tadashi Suzuki, re-devoted themselves to the struggle for the ineluctable truth by means of a radical experimentation based upon 'hard work, punishing exercises, even psychic turmoil. These were the markers, indeed perhaps guarantors, of the distance from commercialism.'[23] It was this path that Lindy Davies fashioned for the School of Drama: 'I wanted to create a place where the sort of people I had worked beside in Brook's company could be trained.' Borrowing the term from psychologist Karl Rogers, she called her model a 'conflict model', that is to say, the creative freedom of the individual actor built upon tightly-constructed rigours of skills training. She and her high-quality staff wove together the twin objectives that had been pulling at the School for decades: a new classicism with the possibility of original work. Training of this intensity, however, comes at a cost, both financial and personal. In the early years of the new century, when things started to get really tough financially, when student numbers grew and staff numbers fell, when space usage was constrained and timetables tightened, the sheer demands of the program became increasingly difficult to maintain. Moreover, other factors were coming to bear that brought into question the future relevance of the kind of training on offer. These factors are brought into relief by the direction of the second path.

If the first path was strongly identified with Lindy Davies, the second has come to be identified with her successor, Kristy Edmunds. Edmunds is from North America and received her training in theatre and film on the West Coast. The tradition she holds dear, then, is not the pyramidal structure of European theatre and dance, but the more horizontally organized centres such as Black Mountain College in North Carolina of the 1940s and '50s, where the training was extensive rather than intensive, the student developed a learning path that suited their own needs, and the art created was not pursuing essential truths, but intent on new horizons. With its widely-based adjunct faculty of practising artists, the learning at Black Mountain was in fact closer to that of an apprenticeship than an institutionalized studentship. And for Edmunds that distinction is a critical one:

> To me the thing about really honest training is that there is a space, there is time, there are tools, there are spirited individuals around that you can work with, so that you can try and try and try. [...] The focus in Performing Arts at the VCA has been on how to train reasonably proficient technicians

of the forms. That means that they will be actors or dancers, but they won't necessarily be creating work. The technician approach develops an attitude of entitlement in the profession and that is a very problematic circumstance, and the sooner conceptual depth, rigour and intent are introduced, the sooner we get thorough performers of material as opposed to technicians undertaking someone else's idea. [...] Arts training has become arts education and that is [not the same as either] the handing down of skills from one generation to another, [or] apprenticeships. I think that the institutionalizing of it is one of the problems.

Kristy Edmunds was appointed to head up the new School of Performing Arts, which combined the previous Schools of Dance, Production and Theatre into a larger unit more able to flex its muscles in the era of takeovers. Her vision was for a school with less emphasis upon 'nurturing' the students and more time and space provided for young artists to try and fail in the creation of their own work. She saw it as a new pedagogy for the new century, one that replaced the traditional model of pre-programmed essential skills followed by productions with a more open weave that provided students with intensive master classes on skills that they sought, and professional feedback when they requested, but which otherwise left them alone to 'get on with it'. It was a form of training closer to the Art School model, and certainly closer to the model articulated by Lenton Parr, which was discussed earlier. It would need a more mobile staff set-up, with room allowed for the input of inspiring artists-in-residence. It would need the money to make this possible; but it would put the VCA on the map internationally as a centre for research into new performance.

Unfortunately, Edmunds arrived at the College just as it was undergoing the process of amalgamation, and she never had the chance to see her vision realised:

> There had been many years of protracted change with resources diminishing for teaching. [...] So, by the time I got there few of the academics were willing to risk losing what little they had.

And, moreover, students were highly sensitive to the motives behind such a radical change in the nature of the training process. The tradition that they expected to be upheld when they entered the Theatre Department—despite Edmunds' view of them as belonging to a generation that 'likes to skin their knees'—was one of close staff attention, intensive skills training and a priority given to strong, secure texts, so that they could focus upon the craft of acting, not the unknown, knee-skinning territory of original work. The Dance students shared a similar expectation. They were more aware of what they might be losing than of what they could gain.

So Edmunds' planned path was buried under the quagmire of amalgamation and all the fear it created. It was a path planned conceptually with great care; it fell foul when it came to implementation. It is not, however, a path that can be ignored. Edmunds came to the job from four years as artistic director of the Melbourne International Festival of the Arts; she left the VCA to become the director of a new multi-arts complex in New York. She is alive to the performance forms that have international currency, and have had currency for several decades. What she sought was a similar currency for the training at the VCA. It will be fascinating to see how the Schools of the VCA face the challenge of remaining 'agents of modernity' and stay ahead of the game into the coming decades of the new century. There are healthy signs, in the curriculum review that is under way as I write, that Edmunds' voice has not gone totally unheard.

2

Culture and community

I have alluded several times to the distinctive culture and community that exists at the VCA. Being a multi-arts training college gives it enormous potential, but it also makes it an extremely complex organization. Each art form conducts very specific forms of training, sets up particular expectations and loyalties in its students, and each has very specific essential needs in terms of equipment, space, time and mix of staff. The challenge, then, has always been how to give practical life to the potential of the VCA community, how to maintain the strength of School tribal bonding while holding together the community of which these tribes are all part. The potential for meaningful interaction between the art forms was envisioned in the original Educational Specifications:

> The propinquity of the various Schools will engen-
> der interdisciplinary exchanges of skills and ideas. It

may be that quite novel marriages of the arts could derive in time. At least it is certain that ways will open for staff and students alike to participate in and appreciate areas of aesthetic experience other than their own.[24]

This was never intended to supplant the central focus upon specific arts training. But there was belief that it was at the edges of the disciplines, where the arts merge into one another, that the interesting work might be created.

For Andrea Hull, this vision of the larger community was more than a matter of artistic predilection; it went to the heart of the identity of the place. She admitted the need for a 'core of purity', but believed that the really exciting work happened 'at the edges':

> It wasn't that I wanted artists to be a bit of every-thing. I wanted a choreographer, for instance, to realize that even a nascent understanding of other languages might enrich their own art form. All of that was part of the edge that we had as a brand. We had this particular capability that no one else had.

This aspect of the original vision for the College has never been fully realized. The question has always been how to draw the community together in ways that will have meaning for the separate parts, in the face of considerable resistance from those staff and students who saw 'hybridity' as a soup without distinctive taste. I think the mistakes have been either to fear interdisci-plinarity as a form of imposed multi-skilling, in which artists would be deprived of time for the development and practice of their own art, or else to fear the loss of individual voice in the messy act of collaboration. The former fear is unfounded: as many examples of interactivity between individual artists, particularly at the postgraduate level, have demonstrated, the opportunity presented is to complement one's own artistic skills with those of artists committed to the same conceptual exploration. For the individual artist involved in this, there can be no loss; nor will there be a gain every time, but when there is, horizons will open and new treasures will be revealed. The act of collaboration does indeed involve practice and a skill set that may lie outside the parameters of specific arts training; but from the point of view of the art created, it is a skill set whose practice is vital. The work on show year after year on the international festival circuit attests to the vibrancy of art created by the interplay between artists from various art forms. At the VCA, there is a ready-made laboratory for this work 'at the edges'.

Faced with the lack of movement from the Schools in developing work from the College community, in 1998 Andrea Hull assembled a Review Panel, with Ken Robinson as Chair, to investigate just those areas of potential that remained unrealized. Apart from reinforcing the need for high-quality specialist training, the Panel made a number of recommendations in response to the perceived 'rapidly changing cultural context', within which they would be practising. One was to do with interdisciplinarity. While not suggesting compulsion, the Panel strongly recommended that a knowledge of other arts forms would better prepare students for changing economic and artistic circumstances. The other area had to do with the breadth of understanding necessary for a contemporary arts practitioner. This recommendation sought some inclusion of art theory in the courses, not 'theoretical courses divorced from practice, but a deeper understanding of the interrelationships of theory in practice'. And it also recognized the 'important place for contextual studies, [...] learning about what being an artist means in this culture and in other cultures'.[25]

The result was the establishment of the Centre for Ideas (CFI), with the apparent objective of trying to fulfil both of the key Curriculum Audit recommendations. Weekly CFI sessions were to be mandatory for all undergraduates, thereby becoming the first element of curriculum common to every VCA student. So as to maximize the opportunities for fruitful cross-disciplinary communication, students from all the Schools would be intermixed in these sessions. Existing theoretical or critical studies in individual Schools would be replaced or complemented with theoretical courses that covered all the arts, thereby exposing the students to the ideas that drove other art forms. These arts-theory courses would be situated within a wider context of socio-cultural thought. Finally, the program would require cross-collaborative practical work between small interdisciplinary groups.

These were ambitious aims, too ambitious perhaps. Again it was not a question of the vision, but of its implementation. In seeking to act as both a spur to cross-collaboration and a conduit for theoretical discourse, the CFI was taking on too much. In the early days, the theory taught was seen as dense and removed from practical artistic concerns, and this in turn tainted its role as a channel for cross-collaboration. On the other hand, the imposition of cross-collaboration flew in the face of the vision of 'non-compulsory' interdisciplinarity articulated in both the Parr and the Robinson documents. The Centre has tried valiantly to adapt to student needs and requests, but without real success.

The die was cast; and CFI is being disbanded. It did put some runs on the board, however: the concept of a community of working artists was at its heart and it did initiate some lasting cross-arts partnerships. But the lesson would seem to be that it is tricky to impose such ventures top down. Preferably, they should emerge out of the Schools themselves—as has happened intermittently over the years: enthusiastic students demanding opportunities to interconnect across the disciplines, and inspirational new-generation staff building into their curricula the stimulus, encouragement and opportunity for this interconnection to happen.

Since 2002 there has existed at the VCA a model of how a community might work that crosses the boundaries of art and forges links that are to do not with personal training, but with a wider and deeper bonding that emerges from identity and culture. Under the indefatigable leadership of Michelle Evans, the Wilin Centre for Indigenous Arts and Cultural Development was a home away from home for Indigenous students enrolled in the programs of the various art schools. The small portable hut in which the Centre was located, and the native garden and fireplace designed by Evans, operated as a base to which the Indigenous students could return when they needed to. But it also became the centre of an energy field and a deep pulse that spread throughout the College. A paragraph from the Wilin Centre website captures the quality of its spirit:

> The Wilin Centre for Indigenous Arts and Cultural Development nurtures and encourages Indigenous artists to achieve their creative potential, while educating the broader student and staff body to recognise the diversity of Australian Indigenous arts and culture. 'Wilin' means 'fire' in the Woi

> Wurrung language. Fire is symbolic to the staff and students of the Wilin Centre—it represents our burning artistic and creative passion. We seek to fan the creative flames and encourage a new generation of Indigenous artists to study and hone their skills through the VCA and Music.[26]

The Wilin Centre was envisioned by Andrea Hull as a vehicle for deeper understanding between white and Indigenous arts practice. In Michelle Evans, this aspect of its charter had a strong advocate, but it is a mistake to think that she succeeded fully in addressing the issue. There was resistance, apathy and misunderstanding in different sectors across the campus, and her plans to install study of Indigenous Australian art practice in the Schools' curricula only partially succeeded. While it was operating strongly as a centre, however, there was progress and hope that some meaningful exchanges could occur. With Evans's departure—under the strain of opposition from the VCA executive in 2009–10—the Centre, its energy, its sense of place, and its fire have been severely diminished. It will be a marker of the VCA's health if the fire can be rekindled in some form, and sooner rather than later.

3

The period of struggle

A more detailed chronology of key stages in the struggle

2005   Federal Minister for Education Brendan Nelson introduces 'cluster' system of funding higher education. VCA faces 35% cut in revenue.

2005–7   Andrea Hull and senior members of VCA Council make repeated attempts to obtain direct Federal and/or State funding for VCA.

Nov 2005   'Heads of Agreement in respect of the Integration of VCA and University of Melbourne' signed by both parties. First attempt to set out broad principles of possible integration.

Nov 2006   Nelson instructs University to fund the shortfall in VCA funding. University at first holds out, but finally agrees, providing VCA amalgamates fully.

Jan 2007   VCA becomes a Faculty of the University of Melbourne.

Aug 2007   University Report on Review of Music recommends amalgamation of VCA School of Music and University Faculty of Music.

2008   Andrea Hull decides to resign as Director of VCA. Decision announced March 2009.

Apr 2009   VCA and Faculty of Music merge into Faculty of VCA and Music. Sharman Pretty becomes Dean of the new Faculty.

12 Apr 2009 Dean Pretty announces in an interview with the *Age* that the Melbourne Model would be applied to VCA, that there would be major budget cuts, and that the VCA's name would change.

late Apr 2009 SaveVCA formed by Ros Walker and other staff and students in the Film and TV School; joined by Scott Dawkins of Music Theatre course. It spreads throughout the VCA.

May 2009   Dean announces axing of the Puppetry program in the School of Performing Arts, and the new Music Theatre course. This causes outcry.

5 June 2009 In an interview with the *Australian* Dean Pretty publicly attacks aspects of previous pedagogy of the VCA.

16 Aug 2009 Save VCA Week launched. A protest march in the city is supported by Noni Hazlehurst, Geoffrey Rush, Hugo Weaving and others.

26 Aug 2009 A letter of concern signed by every living former State arts minister makes a front-page headline in the *Age*. They meet with University Vice-Chancellor Glyn Davis.

Sept 2009   Ted Baillieu, then State Opposition Leader, pledges to support VCA financially, if he were to win office at 2010 election.

Nov 2009   V-C Davis and Dean Pretty release 'Defining the Future: A Discussion Paper for VCAM and the University of Melbourne'. Outlines various ways forward. Review Committee set up, with Ziggy Switkovski as Chair.

Feb-May 2010	Switkovski Committee meets, receives submissions from various sides of the debate, conducts interviews with staff, students and others.
May 2010	Switkovski Committee Report released. Suggests separation of VCAM into two divisions—VCA and Music—under overall Faculty structure within the University; Music to proceed in accordance with the Melbourne Model, VCA to postpone its introduction 'pending further consultation'.
June 2010	University releases a response paper to the Switkovski Report endorsing all the major recommendations.
July 2010	Sharman Pretty resigns as Dean.
July 2010	State Premier John Brumby declares support for VCA. Election due.
Aug 2010	Su Baker, then Head of School of Art, appointed Head of VCA.
Dec 2010	Barry Conyngham, Australian composer and academic, appointed new Dean of Faculty of VCA and Music.

In 2005, the Federal Minister for Higher Education, Science and Training, Brendan Nelson, introduced a radical reform to tertiary-education funding. He placed all the various areas of study into separate funding 'clusters', which would apply across the board in every Australian university. As seems to happen in such moves, funds tended to be 'equalized' downwards rather than upwards. The cluster into which the VCA was placed effectively cut the College's funding from government by 35 per cent, which, as SaveVCA put it, was 'a devastating blow to an institution whose courses were by nature of the practical training, expensive'.[27]

VCA Director Andrea Hull, and senior members of the VCA Council, attempted frantically to find a way to avert the 'devastation'. They approached key ministers in both the State and the Federal governments, arguing the case for the unique standing of the VCA, and its need for a level of funding appropriate to the elite training it offered. There was a concerted attempt to attach the College to the Arts Training Roundtable group of institutions,[28] all of which were directly funded from the Arts Ministry rather than the Ministry of Education. According to Hull, this move was blocked by existing members of the Roundtable, who feared that the size of the VCA would completely skew the funding balance. One might reasonably ask why the VCA did not launch a campaign of public and media support at this point. As Hull recalls it, the Federal Arts Minister, Rod Kemp, promised to find a solution to the VCA's difficulties, providing the College didn't involve the media. Influential supporters were writing letters of support to the minister, but beyond that the gamble was taken that Kemp would come through with the goods. As Hull said, 'Politicians hate any publicity. You have to calculate whether the hate is going to force them further into the burrow or cause them to change.'

All negotiations proved futile, and in late 2006 Nelson instructed the University of Melbourne, with whom the VCA was already affiliated, to fund the $5.3 million shortfall. This was, in the words of Andrea Hull, 'a diabolical solution' and placed both institutions in an invidious position. Both had already entered into a Heads of Agreement in early 2006 as a testing of the waters of what might come to pass. Looking down the barrel of Nelson's gun, the

University at first baulked, but, in the end, agreed to come through with the money, providing the VCA amalgamated fully with the University and became a Faculty under its jurisdiction. The VCA became a Faculty on 1 January 2007.

Had this administrative rearrangement been all, perhaps the amalgamation would have proceeded with less difficulty. Vice-Chancellor Glyn Davis certainly argued convincingly to staff, students and the public at the time of the merger that all great universities should have great arts-training academies connected to them, and that he saw the VCA as potentially 'the jewel in the crown' of the University. However, impacting upon the nature of the amalgamation were four key issues. These became central points of tension in the ensuing struggle.

1. The Melbourne Model

In 2005, the University of Melbourne launched a radical new approach to higher education under the general title of Growing Esteem, since known as the 'Melbourne Model'. Its logo was a triple helix and its vision was for 'a tightly wrapped spiral of distinct but related activities that together define the institution's character'.[29] The three activities so-related were Research, Teaching & Learning, and Knowledge Transfer. The most challenging, controversial and problematic of these was Teaching & Learning, since in the attempt to position itself as a major global centre for graduate study, and therefore Research, the plan was to offer a significantly reduced number undergraduate courses, to be combined into large generalist study areas, from which those students who wanted specialist training would then move into areas of graduate specialization—Law, Medicine, Economics, Architecture or whatever. The Melbourne Model has received a lot of discussion in all forms of media and I do not want to rehearse the debate here. The vision of a breadth of education followed by a depth of specialist training may be a laudable one, and I personally agree with the underlying concept. But on the ground, within the University, it caused academic and administrative chaos, high levels of stress among both staff and students, and a degree of cynicism and concern in the public at large. A number of adjustments have since been made to the original model, and the radical nature of the reform has been somewhat modified.

Now, all this was going on at exactly the time that negotiations were under way for the VCA to amalgamate with the University. Not only was the prospect one of exchanging a large degree of independence for absorption into the University system, but also of deciding whether to join an (untested) educational program that would delay specific artistic training until the graduate level, for which a three-year generalist degree in 'the arts' was required as a pre-requisite, All the Schools at the VCA cried out against this imposition upon their carefully constructed training curriculum. In particular, the Dance School faced the prospect of a three-year gap in the intense physical training that their incoming students had had throughout secondary school.

The University sent out mixed messages. Professor Davis, playing soft cop, asserted that there was no need for the VCA to join the Melbourne Model, and, in an email to students in early 2007, Andrea Hull said that 'no final decisions ha[d] been made'. However, a tougher stance was taken by some of the other high-level negotiators from the University, warning that as a Faculty of the University, the College would have to accept the system. Those of us in charge of curriculum development received a series of deadlines for plans for a new curriculum, to be implemented at first in 2009, later delayed to 2011. In an attempt to work out how we could adjust curriculum without losing the core of the training, we hurried through a range of models. Some of these drafts gained a wider distribution and formed part of the material that the SaveVCA campaign proffered as evidence of a watering down of the pedagogy. Curriculum reviews continue as I write, drawing less explosive responses as the heat of battle diminishes.

The imposition of the Melbourne Model proved to be a major factor in the struggle that arose during 2009. It threatened to compromise the integrity and quality of the artistic training that the VCA offered, and it seemed to provide ready proof of the underlying concerns that joining the University would 'academi-cise' the practical, immersive training that young VCA artists desired and expected.

2. Musical chairs

Organizationally, the most complex problem that the University of Melbourne faced during the period of integration with the VCA was how to deal with the two music schools it now controlled. The Faculty of Music was one of the University's oldest, established in the late nineteenth century. The School of Music at the VCA was the second of the Schools at the College, established in 1975. It is ironic that, according to Noel Denton, VCA Music was originally developed from the

Faculty of Music's Diploma in Music Performance, when the Faculty wanted to off-load the Diploma and focus its attention upon Composition and Musicology. With amalgamation, the University faced the problem of the co-existence of two fully established Music courses. The Review of Music undertaken in August 2007 put the problem succinctly:

> In terms of academic programs and public rela-
> tions, it has become a source of confusion for the
> general community to understand the situation of
> a Bachelor of Music (BMus) being offered through
> the Faculty of Music while there is also a Bachelor
> of Music Performance (BMusPerf) offered through
> the VCA School of Music.

The negotiations around this issue absorbed a good deal of energy and time during the integration process. The 2007 Review recommended that a 'single new school of music should be established with a suite of academic programs based in one principal location'.[30] But disagreements arose over the focus of the new school, the location of premises and the name of the faculty within which it would sit. In brief, the Faculty of Music had already begun a New Generation Degree under the Melbourne Model, whereas the School of Music, as part of the VCA, had not committed one way or the other. This raised concerns at the College that, given the Melbourne Model Music degree, there were 'very strong signs [that] the remaining degrees would also come into line with the MM'.[31]

There was serious disagreement too about the preferred location for the new combined school: in Southbank together with the other arts-training schools, or at Parkville, on the University campus. The upshot is a ridiculous division of the new Music School into two completely discrete units, one at Parkville, one at Southbank. Although, as we have seen, Mark Pollard, Head of the new VCA Music program, sees some definite advantages in it, this separation would appear to confirm all the worst fears about the impossibility of a true integration.

Finally, the matter of the new Faculty's name provoked a series of head-on boardroom battles. The VCA had always assumed 'Music', as included under its rubric of 'the Arts'. On the other hand, the Faculty of Music had a name, a history and a tradition that they were not happy about losing. In the end a compromise name was hammered out: The Faculty of VCA and Music, or VCAM. Both sides lost their treasured brand, and neither was happy with the new one. For SaveVCA and all those fighting for the survival of the College's identity the loss of name was iconoclastic, and indicative of all the other losses they feared would eventuate.

3. Give 'em enough [financial] rope ...

The VCA had been in financial difficulties long before the 2005 Nelson reforms and the 2006 ultimatum to the University of Melbourne. The draft of the Director's Issues Paper, delivered to the first VCA leadership retreat on 3 February 1998, begins with the following overview:

> The VCA council is aware that the VCA faces profound financial and organizational challenges. As part of the higher education sector it faces a contraction of at least 17% in purchasing power of grant funding over 4 years. However, unlike the rest of the higher-education sector it does not generate

substantial research income, it relates to a poverty-stricken industry and profession and is unable to attract recurrent funds from relevant government departments. It has no substantial disposable assets, no reserves to fund risk-taking new product developments.

The introduction to the paper concludes that 'the situation is grim and the prospects not optimistic'.[32]

The late 1980s and the 1990s saw a reversal of the large increases in governmental expenditure on tertiary education over the previous decades: 'The 1998–2000 Triennium Higher-Education Funding Report projected that federal funding will account for less than half of higher education by the year 2000 compared with the 1988 figure of 75%.'[33]

The 1998 Issues Paper attributed the cause of this reversal of funding firmly to the question of 'accountability':

As the outlay [of the previous decades] represents a significant proportion of public-sector expenditure, there has been a sharp increase in accountability viz, satisfactory and acceptable stewardship by the tertiary sector for use of this public money.

The spreading behemoth of 'accountability' has been unstoppable over the past decade. As Anthony Grigg says, it has 'gone beyond the point of common sense.

I'm not sure that [a critical financial situation] is an issue just for arts education. I think it's also an issue for higher education more generally. It is getting so bogged down now in accountability, [that it] has gone beyond the point of common sense. It's not about not being accountable; it's about What's the balance? The dollars are being stretched so far—particularly here in Australia and it is happening in the UK again—that this is a sector reaching a breaking point.

Accountability finds its way into all aspects of artistic and educational endeavour, hovering, like a superego, ready to challenge the legal, the safety, the ethical and, of course, the financial aspects of any activity, on behalf of that easily referenced but ill-defined figure, 'the taxpayer'. 'The prime pressure on governments', notes the 1998 Paper, is 'to demonstrate to taxpayers that funds are being spent efficiently and in so doing are producing a desirable and competitive society.'[34] Surely, this was written with the tongue planted firmly in the cheek. A society defined as 'desirable' in relation to its 'efficient' spending of funds and its 'competitiveness' would seem to me to be one devoted to consumerism. The effect of mixing arts and arts training with consumerism is one that I have already touched upon.

The three-point survival strategy that Andrea Hull put to the leaders' retreat in 1998 was 'to grow, to save and/or to cut'.

To grow

Given the ceiling on Commonwealth-supported places for undergraduate students, the only growth areas were in domestic fee-paying students, to which the VCA had strong ethical objections, or in international fee-paying students, or various forms of philanthropy, but, as Anthony Grigg said, 'neither was ever going to generate enough money to solve the problem'. The postgraduate area, which has grown exponentially over the past decade, is also a money-spinner, but it brings with it its own problems in terms of space and support. Non-degree evening courses became significant revenue streams, in particular in the Drama School and the Music School.

To cut

The heads of schools were averse to the alternative of cutting programs—and therefore staff. And, in truth, on the floor we were all working long hours with minimal staff numbers, attempting to maintain high-level training courses, most of which were not made up of modular units that could be cut out with little effect. Arts training is a person-to-person process: a generational handing down of skills and techniques, and a finely modulated stimulation and encouragement of creative endeavour and imaginative transformation. It does not operate on the level of the transmission of packages of knowledge. It takes place in studios and ateliers. It cannot be taught in lecture halls to classes of 500 students.

It was disappointing, therefore, to have Glyn Davis—whose initial vision of the 'great arts-training faculty' seemed like a haven of escape from governments devoted to 'accountability'—writing in 2009, after the merger, of the need to address 'the Faculty's average student:staff ratio, which is the lowest of all the University of Melbourne faculties'.[35] Accountability seems to be inescapable. It is interesting to place Professor Davis's comment alongside the observation made by Professor Don McLean, Dean of the Schulich School of Music at McGill University in Canada, who had been an external member of the Music Review Panel in 2007:

> The current full-time academic staffing cohort of the combined schools [of Music] falls short of the complement typical of the international benchmark

institutions with which the new school would hope to compare itself, and the University would therefore need to continue to take a leadership position in advocating for appropriate tertiary-education funding levels to sustain excellence in the media, fine arts, and performing-arts programs, including music, for which it is now responsible.[36]

If Professor Davis truly believes that the VCA should be the 'jewel in the crown' of the University, bright enough to continue attracting the best students, the University needs to take that leadership position and to ensure a requisite staff:student ratio and a standard of staff employed to keep the shine on the jewel. Arts training cannot be done on the cheap. The financial difficulties facing the VCA over the years have had relatively little to do with bad financial management. As Andrea Hull says, 'We were a very lean little outfit.' The fact is that both art and arts training require substantial financial support from governments. This in turn requires a commitment to them as having worth that cannot be measured in terms of accountability. If the support is not sufficient, then the rope offered will be long enough only for them to hang themselves with.

To save

Over the decade following 1998, the main action taken to save funds was in the area of the centralization of administrative functions. This process removed administrative power from the individual schools, where it had historically been placed, and put it in the hands of a growing central bureaucracy, which struggled to keep in touch with the specific needs of each training area. Undoubtedly, there were advantages to this re-structuring, in terms of the efficiency needed in the administration of an organization of growing complexity; but since amalgamation the process has continued apace, to the point where there is very little interplay between the bureaucracy and the arts training. Moreover, the whole issue of financial savings has been turned on its head since amalgamation. An administration that was running at about 23 per cent of the budget immediately prior to the merger is now running at close to 50 per cent. Grigg was right: this is 'beyond the point of common sense'. To make matters worse, the University, forced by the government to subsidize VCA by $4 million, is charging the VCA $6 million in rent for land and premises that previously belonged to the VCA.[37]

The VCA was not financially well-off before the Nelson reforms, yet it was surviving—thanks to careful management, efficient use of resources, enterprise, marketing, hard work and commitment to the base focus of person-to-person training. The cuts to funding that followed as a result of university funding 'clusters' would have tipped the College over the edge of survival. Andrea Hull is precise in her reading of the decision: 'The deals were political; they had nothing to do with pedagogy or need. [...] If you are a federal bureaucrat, you don't go into the niceties of nuanced training.'

This financial tipping-point, its potential effects upon the standards of 'nuanced training', and the effects of the increasing bureaucratization of the system, were all key issues in the struggle of 2009–10.

4. Who's at First Base?

Whatever plans for change one tries to introduce at a curricular, administrative or larger organizational level, whether or not these succeed will depend, in an institution as finely balanced as the VCA, almost entirely upon the quality of the people in charge at each level of implementation. It is not as if the VCA had been in benign stasis over the preceding years. When I reflect upon the constantly shifting political directions, and the countless new plans for change and improvement we were obliged to implement over my decades of involvement at the VCA, the words of the Beatles always come to mind:

> You say you got a real solution
> Well, you know
> We'd all love to see the plan.
> You ask me for a contribution
> Well, you know
> We're all doing what we can.[38]

Many experts were brought in during the process of amalgamation with the University to aid with the stages of this upheaval. They all observed that the VCA staff were in a state of 'change fatigue'. As artists, or people committed to the arts, most of the staff are not averse to change; the state of art is one of constant change. But 'the plan' that 'we'd all love to see' is a vision for the new future direction. It is not sufficient to argue for financial exigency or management efficiency or bureaucratic need. We need an inspiring vision and sense of purpose.

The VCA began its life under the leadership of the inspirational Lenton Parr, an artist, a tough negotiator, a leader who knew how to decentralize the tasks of leading without losing control. Parr wrought the embryonic VCA from the century-old National Gallery of Victoria Arts School in 1973 and presided over the addition of the Schools of Music (1974), Drama (1975), and Dance (1979). His founding educational charter, the 'Educational Specifications for The Victorian College of the Arts', provided the blueprint for the development of a unique institution over the subsequent ten years.

Parr left the VCA in 1984 and, after an interregnum of less than inspiring leadership, his mantle was assumed by Andrea Hull in 1995. Hull is not herself an artist, but, during her time at the Australia Council and as Chief Executive of the Western Australian Department for the Arts, had devoted her working life to the support and promotion of the arts. In other words, she came to the VCA as a successful arts bureaucrat, and, although there is some argument that her lack of direct connection to artistic practice limited her thinking when faced with some of the problems outlined in this essay, there is no doubt that she brought to the College an unflagging energy and a sense of vision that shaped a golden period in its history. In a sense, the fact that she wasn't an artist gave her a breathing space from the micro-problems of any one School and allowed her to maintain a healthy overview of the College as a whole. She was a tireless promoter and was successful in raising the VCA profile by setting up a marketing division, and by her own advocacy of financial support from philanthropists as much as from the public purse. She broadly re-organized the internal structures of the College administration—not always a popular move—and fought to keep the ship in balance as storms rocked it from all sides. Most especially, in the VCA itself she kept a high profile. She was seen to care: she talked openly to students and to staff; she witnessed their work at arts shows, music recitals, performances, and film showings. She asserted constantly that the real pay-off for her work was the ability to see the artwork that emerged from this multi-disciplinary campus.

Hull resigned from the VCA just as the ink was drying on the amalgamation document. She had fought long and hard to keep the College as an independent institute. Her health was not strong at the time and she had other personal challenges she wished to take up. But it is hard to believe that the failure of her endeavour to keep the VCA under its own charter had not taken all the winds out of her sails. The shore that she saw the VCA approaching was not the one she had struggled against the storms to reach. Looking back, her view of the amalgamation process is vivid and incisive:

> Most mergers and takeovers in the corporate world have key features, and they're not dissimilar in any not-for-profit or university world either—and the key features are that the dominant culture will prevail and the dominant culture has a whole pile of elements to it. In history, colonizers were either benign or brutal. If they were brutal, they wiped out the language, they enslaved the people, they destroyed the iconographic, emotional heartland by destroying the monuments or whatever. [In 2010 Lenton Parr's iconic pentagram was replaced with the emblem of the University of Melbourne.] If they were benign, they let certain things flourish. So you've got to step back and think, 'What are these things about?' They're not necessarily acts of benign charity.

Andrea Hull's replacement, Sharman Pretty, hardly stood a chance. By the time she walked onto the field the battlelines had already been drawn. Unfortunately, she acted like a magnet, drawing onto herself all the frustrations, fears, anger and disappointments felt and expressed by the staff, the students and the members of the public who were fighting against the 'fall' of the VCA. If the University was too diffuse a body upon which to heap calumny, if the Vice-Chancellor and his deputies were too skilled at 'spin' and too removed for direct combat, if, indeed, the historical difficulties of the VCA with regard to financial and administrative survival were too embedded to make a clear target, then *someone* had to be made to wear the mask of Darth Vader: a good cause needs a clear enemy target to aim at. In short, if Professor Pretty had not happened along, we would have had to invent her.[39]

Professor Pretty was the first head of the VCA chosen primarily by the University. It is clear, therefore, that the University must have given her a brief to navigate the financial straits the College was in and to prepare it for entry into the Melbourne Model. These directives were already sure to involve decisions bound to be unpopular with a large percentage of students and staff. So, to some degree her path was charted for her.

Nevertheless, it has to be said that if there were mistakes to be made that were certain to engender confusion, dismay and distrust, Professor Pretty made them—not just in what she chose to do in order to make the College 'accountable', but also in how she chose to go about doing it. These mistakes were largely to do with questions of leadership style, or the lack thereof: not communicating, perhaps not having, a vision for the exciting possibilities of new direction; not giving herself the time to get to know the College and the wider Melbourne arts scene, thereby misjudging the nature of its culture, making misguided cuts, and underestimating the level of reaction they would occasion; and perhaps most tellingly, not communicating or discussing the rationale for her actions with the students and the staff—setting up, in fact, what was seen as a wall of isolation between her and the College community. As I have outlined, significant changes had to be made. In fact, the College is still in the process of implementing those changes.

I have tried to argue in this essay that these changes have as much to do with the necessities of adjusting to the shifting directions for arts training that are relevant in the new century, as with the changing circumstances of power. There is also little doubt that there was a great deal of resistance within the VCA to the kind of curricular and organizational moves that were necessary. But strong leadership was vital during the process of changeover; it was an opportunity for a new dean to present a charter that made the running in both areas. Unfortunately, the charter presented by Professor Pretty was not convincing, with the result that she was seen as 'just a wrecker', who had no vision 'other than to asset-strip to balance the budget', to quote some of the descriptors heard at the time.

In the upshot, she became the scapegoat. In the spotlight of public scrutiny and media attacks, she was put under relentless pressure. Sharman Pretty finally resigned when the Switkowski Report, which the University accepted, included an implicit critique of her methods of operation.[40] There can be no doubt that these methods provided a target for anger, and they brought matters to a head. Her resignation proved to be a gesture of considerable significance. For Ros Walker of SaveVCA, the replacement of Sharman Pretty with Su Baker was one of the four key achievements of the campaign: 'We now have a dean who is a respected practitioner, and who is going to be sympathetic to the way in which artists are trained.'

Conclusion
The way forward

Questions of leadership style are always fundamental to the way in which an organization copes with large-scale change. For an organization whose culture has been brutally challenged, the leader needs to proceed with caution and sensitivity, but also with vigour. In Su Baker the VCA is fortunate to have someone who can work from within its community. She is herself an artist and brings to her role a thorough understanding of the path necessary for deep training at both the core and interdisciplinary levels. She is a pragmatist, and she is both willing and able to work within the newly defined VCA structure, seeing it as a 'necessary stage' to be gone through in order to 'restore the spirit, the home base' and then to 'become more inventive'. The task she has enthusiastically undertaken is to bring about the restoration of confidence in both staff and students, and a reinvigoration of a culture that had been nurtured over thirty years.

The vigorous growth of the VCA, however, is not dependent on the actions of a single individual, no matter how well-equipped she might be for the task.

It depends upon the institute acquiring—and being accorded—a sufficient degree of independent power that will enable it to deal with the challenges it will have to face as it adapts to changing circumstances. Throughout this essay I have proposed, implicitly and explicitly, means by which the institute might develop a healthy constitution. That the VCA deserves to prosper seems to me—as it does to all those who sustained the campaign in 2009 and 2010—beyond question. So let me conclude by drawing together the principal threads of my argument, and itemizing what a syllabus handbook might refer to as the 'prerequisites for satisfactory progress'.

First, the undertakings of governments, particularly the Baillieu State government, to make adequate provision of funds for the VCA to go forward, confident of its economic stability, must be honoured. Moreover, this funding must be free from the crippling demands of accountability. For its part, the VCA will have to accept that there has to be a 'satisfactory and acceptable stewardship' of these funds—not the imposition of an intolerable degree of administrative scrutiny. Such scrutiny not only makes unreasonable demands upon staff, and clogs the system with needless bureaucracy, but also restricts the freedom of movement and imaginative decision-making that are the hallmarks of a great arts-training academy. Furthermore, there needs to be an easing of accountability in respect of academic and artistic outcomes. While one has every right to expect the training offered to be of the highest standard, it does not follow that that standard should be measured by students' success in securing immediate work, nor by the immediate public acclaim of the work they produce. Artistic ability can be slow to mature: one has no right to expect a new graduate to have already developed a fully-fledged talent. The investment the VCA is making is in the long haul.

Next, the University of Melbourne is going to have to learn that the beast with which it is attempting, somewhat reluctantly, to mate is not as others are. This is not a case of special pleading, and the VCA too, having been taken over, for better or for worse, is going to have to learn to work within a university faculty structure. But it must be acknowledged that the business and needs of the VCA are radically different from those of other, more academic, less professional and practice-based disciplines. It cannot be grafted willy-nilly onto the larger body and be expected to automatically survive the transplant. It needs to be cut a lot of slack, trusted to develop on its own terms, given licence to plan its curricula in accordance with its own culture, and allowed to take greater control of the administration of its own activities. In a word, it needs a generous measure of independence. Only then will it earn the right to be referred to, as Glyn Davis did, as the 'jewel in the University's crown'.

Finally, the VCA must not scurry timidly back to its various burrows and try to carry on as though nothing has happened these past years. Indeed, it's at times of crisis that opportunities for meaningful change can present themselves. Instability, as Kristy Edmunds said, 'can either cause people to collapse [...], or to re-treat [into] anything that's familiar, or it can generate a kind of liberty to pursue a new future.' In setting up his new stream in Contemporary Music, Mark Pollard has seized the opportunity offered by the split in the old Music School. His positive move in a situation that could have been seen as catastrophic has set an example for the VCA as a whole. The challenge that lies ahead is to see the imposition of a new identity, the new organizational framework, the new demands for curricular review as a chance to reconfigure an arts training that is responsive to current debates, debates about questions of artistic principle and educational philosophy relevant to the twenty-first century.

Endnotes

1   *The Complete Poems and Plays of T.S. Eliot* (London: Faber and Faber, 1969), p.109.

2   The poem has it in Latin: 'Quis hic locus, quae regio, quae mundi plaga?'.

3   *Complete Poems*, pp.109, 110.

4   With thanks in part to Joseph Pascoe, *Creating: The Victorian College of the Arts* (Melbourne: Macmillan, 2000) and to SaveVCA, 'Information for Arts and Cultural Tourism Industries' (2009).

5   On the Browne Report, 'Securing a Sustainable Future for Higher Education', see, for instance, S. Collini, 'Browne's Gamble', *London Review of Books*, 4 Nov. 2010.

6   'Educational Specifications', in 'The Victorian College of the Arts' (1974).

7   'The Institution of Training', *Performance Research*, 14. 2 (2009), p.6. This article provides the template for the following brief historical positioning of arts training in relation to the VCA.

8   Shepherd, p.5.

9   Shepherd, pp.7, 8.

10 *Deschooling Society* (Harmondsworth: Penguin, 1973).

11 'Educational Specifications', p.3:1.

12 'Educational Specifications', p.3:2.

13 'Educational Specifications', pp.3-2, 6:1.

14 'Educational Specifications', p.3:3.

15 'Educational Specifications', pp.6:4, 6:5.

16 Interestingly, in his later years as a teacher, after leaving VCA, Oyston became an expert on the methods of Stanislavski.

17 Author's interview with Lindy Davies.

18 Shepherd, p.6.
19 'Skills for Australia', available at http://www.voced.edu.
    au/search/index.php?searchtype=full&quantity=1&d
    ocnum=%22td/lmr+85.648%22&query=SEARCH&
    hitstart=1 (accessed 30 March 2011).
20 'Dawkins' Higher-Education Reforms and how
    Metaphors Work in Policy Making', *Journal of Higher
    Education Policy Management*, 24 (2002), p.88.
21 *The Key Issues concerning Contemporary Art* (Melbourne:
    UniMelb Research School, 2007), pp.177, 31, 49, 118,
    123.
22 *Key Issues*, p.232.
23 Shepherd, p.9.
24 'Educational Specifications', p.3:7.
25 'Curriculum Audit: Report and Recommendations', a
    report to the VCA Council, 15–18 December 1998,
    pp.4, 6.
26 'About the Wilin Centre for Indigenous Arts and
    Cultural Development', available at http://www.vcam.
    unimelb.edu.au/wilin/about (accessed 18 April 2011).
27 'Information for the Arts and Cultural Tourism
    Industries', released by SaveVCA (Nov. 2009), p. 7. For
    a vigorous debate on the pros and cons of the SaveVCA
    case against the Nelson Reform, see the Crikey article
    'Does anybody in Canberra really know anything?' by
    Noel Turnbull, and the Comments section following.
    http://www.crikey.com.au/2010/06/24/come-in-spinner-
    does-anybody-in-canberra-really-know-anything/ (ac-
    cessed 18 April 2011).
28 The group consists of the National Institute of
    Dramatic Art (NIDA), the Australian Film, Television
    and Radio School (AFTRS), the National Institute
    of Circus Arts (NICA), the Australian National
    Academy of Music (ANAM) and the Australian
    Ballet School.
29 'Growing Esteem: The University of Melbourne'
    (2005), p.12.
30 'Report on Review of Music (Aug 2007)', Appendix B

(University of Melbourne, Planning and Budget Committee), pp.1, 3.

31 SaveVCA (2009), p.11.

32 'Director's Issues Paper' (VCA Council, 1998) (draft), p.2.

33 'Director's Issues Paper', p.6.

34 Ibid.

35 'Defining the Future for the VCA and Music at The University of Melbourne: A Discussion Paper' (Nov. 2009), p.25.

36 'Defining the Future for the VCA and Music', p.7. See also the comment by Evan Walker, former minister in the State Government and VCA Council President: 'The critical issue is to avoid putting at risk our international reputation because of the requirements of funding formulas' quoted in *Creating: The Victorian College of the Arts*, ed. by J. Pascoe (Melbourne: Macmillan, 2000), p.55.

37 Figures taken from 'Defining a New and Better Future for the VCA: A Submission to the VCAM Review Panel on behalf of Noel Turnbull, The Hon. Race Mathews, Lynne Landy and Noel Denton' (Feb. 2010), p.13.

38 'Revolution' (Lennon-McCartney). Lyrics available at http://www.songlyrics.com/beatles/revolution-lennon-mccartney-lyrics/ (accessed 20 Mar. 2011).

39 It was my decision not to interview either Professor Davis or Professor Pretty. I was more interested in the ramifications of actions that were taken and of the perceptions of motive and behaviour by the staff and student body than in finding the 'correct' version of the cause of the events. Besides, in situations such as this, there are as many correct versions as there were participants.

40 See 'Report of the Review Committee in Response to the VCAM Discussion Paper' (2010), set up by the Vice-Chancellor in 2009-10 and chaired by Ziggy Switkowski, and 'The Future of Visual and Performing Arts at the University of Melbourne' (2010).

Readers' Forum

Response to Erin Brannigan's *Moving Across Disciplines: Dance in the Twenty-first Century* (Platform Paper 25)

Dr Cheryl Stock was Head of Dance at Queensland University of Technology 2000–06 and is currently Associate Professor. She has served as National President of Audance and Chair of the Dance Board of the Australia Council. As an artist she has created over 50 dance and theatre works and in 2003 received the Lifetime Achievement Award at the Australia Dance Awards for her work as a director, writer and leader in tertiary education.

Whilst there is much rhetoric around the theory of interdisciplinary practice, rarely is there any in-depth critique of what this might mean in the practice itself, particularly in the arts. Erin Brannigan in her paper, *Moving Across Disciplines: Dance in the Twenty-first Century,* could have taken many approaches to dance working in an interdisciplinary context— such as integrating practices and perspectives from health, architecture or cognitive science. She chose, however, an arts-specific focus, with dance firmly at the centre and leading the discussion. Through a thoughtful, knowledgeable and at times provocative historical and philosophical analysis, Brannigan convincingly makes the case for her assertion that 'dance is increasingly the "host" for the most progressive interdisciplinary practices' (p.8). Her wide-ranging overview of dance artists and their work in the twentieth century—problematising the shifts around current somatic dance practices, highly stylised theatrical traditions and much in between—informs insightful discussion on how key conceptual underpinnings (what Brannigan calls 'the creative operations of interdisciplinary practice') are grounded in embodied disciplinary compositional processes. These, she argues, form the common ground on which interdisciplinarity rests. The particular working practices and astute observations of choreographers Obarzaneck, Guerin and Herbertson enliven the discussion with their voices, providing perceptive dance-led examples of the highly effective ways in which dance transforms a single art form into an integrated, hybridised interdisciplinary form.

There is, however, an ongoing and predictable tension that Brannigan and these choreographers identify; between the highly-specialised and focussed discipline specificity of dance and the open-ended conceptual, reflexive and creative enquiry necessary for moving across disciplines. This dilemma is also writ large in the section on speculative dance training for this century which embraces and somehow marries both demands.

Even an extended paper cannot hope to provide a comprehensive sweep of the topic of dance and inter-disciplinarity, but in this essay the Melbourne-centric choice of dance artist interviews and the Sydney centric discussion of the particular challenges for dance training in Sydney seem slightly at odds with the more wide-ranging international reach of the early historical over-view. In a twenty-first-century Australian dance context Sue Healey with her live work, film and installations, Garry Stewart and his collaborations with robotics and photography, Gavin Webber and Kate Champion with their mixed-media theatrical productions and Hellen Sky with her ongoing interrogation of generative and interactive performance, could provide other nuanced artist insights of dance moving across disciplines.

Perhaps this musing of omissions merely reflects a desire for more and longer debates and writings around the significance of dance as a leader in interdisciplinary practice, especially in Australia. Erin Brannigan has provided an important catalyst with her considered, complex and persuasive study which is a pleasure to ponder on. It should be on the reading list of every dance and creative arts course and disseminated widely through the industry.

Response to Lenine Bourke and Mary Ann Hunter's *Not Just an Audience: Young People Transforming Our Theatre* (Platform Paper 26)

Sophie Morstyn and Jessica Wotton are Year 12 students at Ascham studying Drama and interested in careers in the theatre.

Not Just an Audience: Young People Transforming Our Theatre, the Platform Paper by Lenine Bourke and Mary Ann Hunter, deals with the issue of integrating young people into the construction of relevant, innovative theatre. Technological advancements have offered a new allure to young audiences that has caused a decrease in attendance at live performances and, as dedicated theatre lovers ourselves, we find this a scary thought. This paper asks the question: why is it that what young people have to offer the arts industry is considered less valuable than what current, established practitioners have to say? Youth has quickly become a 'tick-a-box priority' and our value to the theatre industry is being discounted. This is one of the major issues addressed in the essay. We are particularly interested in the idea that teachers were being taught to use drama as a pedagogical tool, integrating it into the early life of students. Understanding the purpose of drama is vitally important and by experiencing it in early life will lead to a love and appreciation of live performance later on.

However, one of the intriguing ideas raised by the paper is that theatre should be seen as something separate from education. Theatre's original purpose was to engage audiences, not to be an onerous burden on them. It still is, but unfortunately, today young people seem subconsciously to connect theatre to school and therefore find it less appealing. The authors also suggest a way in which this might be fixed: an event should be created around the show. This would mean that there was a more personal engagement with the idea of theatre, the 'theatre community' would be revived and, to tweak the authors' rhetorical question a little, Might not 'young punters camp out to get their tickets to the next state theatre show as they [do] for the next Big Day Out?'

Schools and theatre companies are also attempting to foster a love of theatre by offering students theatre subscriptions and installing programs such as the YAP (Youth Advisory Panel at Sydney Theatre Company). However the essay's point, that in later life this motivation to see live performances diminishes, is valid. As young theatre-goers, we would welcome a cultural and generational shift towards a more collaborative theatre industry, one that embraces more than simply the ideas of established practitioners and artists. One of the proposed ways of making theatre more accessible to younger audiences that we found exciting was that of 'pop up theatre', because we feel that transitional performance spaces would not only add another level to a production, but enable young minds to assist in professional works.

It seems that often theatre companies use established directors, producers or actors for their productions rather than offering the opportunity to younger, less experienced practitioners whose contribution is seen as less valid. At the Sydney launch of the essay, Jennie Bradbury (Babushka Productions) suggested that 'slippers are our (theatre's) biggest competition', meaning that the older theatre community is becoming too comfortable with the current idea of theatre and that they need to embrace the ideas of younger audience members or practitioners, who could help revive the perception of theatre as an engaging experience. *Not Just an Audience* is proof that this transition is happening. People such as Lenine Bourke and Mary Ann Hunter are not only identifying the issues that are preventing youth from joining the theatre community, but also proposing solutions, meaning that, as young theatre lovers, we are being offered more opportunities to get involved and help create the future of theatre in Australia.

Response to Robert Reid's *Hello World! Promoting the Arts on the Web* (Platform Paper 27)

John Bailey is an arts writer for the *Sunday Age*, *RealTime* and other publications. He lectures in the School of Culture and Communication at the University of Melbourne and maintains several websites based around Melbourne arts and culture.

An early section of Robert Reid's *Hello World!* offers a much-needed engagement with the troubled history of archiving in Australian performing arts. 'There's nothing new about the assertion that Australian theatre repeats itself out of ignorance of its cultural heritage,' he says, before going on to unpack one of the great paradoxes of the information age. We often think of online media as ephemeral, without weight or lasting impact. A blog post or tweet is not a book or a clipping that we can store in a vault. Yet with a few keystrokes I can summon up reviews of productions ten years gone, search out the histories of their players, and discover what they're up to today. Though as tangible as sunshine, these electronic records are more accessible, and in their own way enduring, than a fading text locked in a conventional archival institution. Perhaps it's doubly appropriate that theatre, itself such a transient medium, should find an ally in the dispersed and ever-shifting realm of the internet.

But Reid is far from an ecstatic evangelist for the democratising possibilities of new media; as he rightly notes, emergent modes of communication have brought with them new structures of power and accessibility. The internet does offer the potential for new voices to make themselves heard, but not everyone has the particular urge to take up that offer.

While I firmly believe that anyone can write, it often turns out that the pleasures and frustrations of writing attract particular personalities. This is something that applies to both online and more traditional forms of written expression. While Reid suggests that blogs and the like can best be understood along the lines of oral, rather than written, histories, I think there are limits to that notion. If writing of whatever sort is a conversation, it's a peculiar one that evades many of the demands of live discussion while throwing up new limitations of its own.

Any blogger will know the weird sense of beginning an online 'conversation'. It's akin to delivering an informal lecture to an empty auditorium. In most cases, you're met with silence. This is no different from a newspaper review, or a novel, or a message scratched into a bus stop seat. If your thoughts provoke lively debate or passionate exchange, you're not there to be part of it. And while blog posts do enable responses from any and all readers, in practice it's a small minority who feel compelled to add their voice to the mix.

Of course, most writers probably do want to be part of a conversation, but it's a particular kind of dialogue that proceeds at a more controlled pace. Writing is the preparation of ideas in a quiet room, usually in isolation, with enough time (one hopes) to be confident that what's being expressed is close to what one intends. This is a process with a great deal of psychic appeal to those who make it a foundation of their lives; but again, it's not everyone who finds in themselves the need to measure their thoughts out in this way.

My point here is that I think it's no surprise that almost every person blogging on the performing arts in Australia is already a writer of some description. To return to the keyboard again and again despite little reward, to keep starting conversations that never engender a whisper of response, to lecture to that empty auditorium, requires a certain degree of fortitude, if not a masochist streak. And it needs a pay-off that isn't confined to the reciprocal actualisation of identity allowed by genuine interpersonal exchange. We make who we are through our interactions with others, but the form of self-expression afforded by writing is a guarded, partial kind of interaction.

When we move from the longer form of blogs to social networking sites such as Facebook and Twitter, this dynamic does shift. More audiences make use of these to participate in exchanges about the performing arts; but while Reid doesn't address it explicitly, the second half of his essay is haunted by the 'signal to noise' problem of online communications. Useful discussion or analysis can often be lost in torrents of 'OMG best show ever' and undisguised publicity screeds. Very few people re-tweet a bad review of their production, even if it does come in at under 140 characters. While a lot of conversations about theatre end with, 'we really need more dialogue', increased volume doesn't necessarily mean increased quality.

Reid's examination of creative works which themselves involve new media furthers these points: 'The participatory element of social media [...] offers the opportunity to become the performance itself.' But not every audience member wants to be the production, and the responses to some of the works he describes suggest that giving audiences the opportunity to be heard isn't particularly useful if they don't have anything to say.

Just because the Web promises new ways of engaging with the performing arts doesn't mean we should (or can) force people to take these up. Theatre is an offer, not a command. In this light, I particularly like Reid's suggestion of an open source wiki devoted to Australian theatre history, in which a community that chooses to can create a dedicated and self-regulating archival resource. I don't know that we need more 'hubs' that attempt to aggregate everything of interest in the world of the arts—there's simply no way of casting a net that wide, and the growing presence of the arts on the Internet has been enabled not due to concentration but dispersal. Individual blogs die out, users stop checking into Facebook, but none of these are the lynchpins holding together communities. Yet sites that are admittedly incomplete, subject to communal revision and which develop outside of commercial needs would seem to me worth supporting. That's how real conversations work.

James Waites worked in the Australian print media for over twenty years, specialising in theatre reviewing and broader arts commentary. These days he has a theatre website (www.jameswaites.com), financed by his work as an interviewer for the National Library of Australia's Oral History and Folklore unit. He is the author of Platform Paper 23, *Whatever Happened to the STC Actors Company?*

Robert Reid's Platform Paper *Hello World! Promoting the Arts on the Web* covers a fascinating range of topics, but I shall only respond to the one with which I am most directly connected, blogging.

It is clearly of concern that the print media have decided to no longer engage meaningfully in cultural debate in the form of hiring, keeping, protecting, paying and publishing 'qualified' theatre critics. As someone who has been in such employ—at the *National Times* in the 1980s and the *Sydney Morning Herald* in the 1990s—I have enjoyed the privileges and challenges that go with this kind of work. I could wax lyrical on the days when it was not uncommon to be allowed up to 1,000 words for one of my reviews, none of which was touched without my agreement, in newspapers that were read regularly by tens of thousands of people. And look what we have now: Martin Ball has just resigned from the *Age* because he has been told he must restrict himself to a maximum of 250 words. What room is there for anything else after outlining the plot and describing the set? The job could be done by a well-programmed robot.

More disturbing is the cosy relationship between the marketing departments of big arts organizations and the major print media, where there is now an implicit under-standing that income from advertising will have a 'constrain-ing' effect on 'negative' editorial content. I believe that in a very real sense these big companies have helped facilitate the 'death of criticism'. Whatever the imagined short-term gain in silencing potential dissent, in the long term we are left with no history.

Blogging, writing on the 'net', has come along just in time to save the day. But it's not the same. As Reid rightly points out, blogging at this stage in its evolution, is essentially an amateur pursuit—'amateur' in the literal and best sense of the word, done for the love if it.

In the long term, the money factor will have to be faced. Personally, I am happy not to be paid. I enjoy the freedom money can't buy. But I was paid for years as I learned my craft in the print media, as was Alison Croggon, whose outstanding work in the field Reid refers to several times, and most others currently writing interesting theatre blogs in this country. Over the next decade or so this connection with experience and training will die out. Where, after that, will the skilled commentators come from?

I am sure Croggon would agree, blogging also brings new challenges. Because of its interactive nature, it often requires a lot more work per assignment. Croggon's recent review of *Baal* promoted over 90 comments, many from her as she guided the sometimes excited debate away from over-heating. What ensued was a fascinating roller-coaster of an exchange, highlighting all that is good about theatre blogging. It is an easily overlooked fact that writing the initial review online is one thing and managing the debate that follows is quite another. Not just more time, but extra 'people' skills.

I worry about the future. If Australian theatre is going to enjoy good 'criticism' well into this new century, where is it going to come from? What can we do to cultivate an environment from which more good bloggers might emerge? Is it time we started to look at ways of training reviewers? And if so, who is going to take responsibility for that? As for the question of remuneration—well, who knows how that is going to pan out?

Subscribe to **Platform Papers**

Have the papers delivered quarterly to your door

4 issues for $60.00 including postage within Australia

The individual recommended retail price is $14.95.

___ I would like to subscribe to 4 issues of Platform Papers for $60.00

I would like my subscription to start from: ___ this issue (No. 28)

___ the next issue (No. 29)

Name_____

Address_____

_____

_____ State _____ Postcode _____

Email _____

Telephone _____

Please make cheques payable to Currency House Inc.

Or charge: ___ Mastercard ___ Visa

Card no. ___ ___ ___ ___ ___ ___ ___ ___ ___ ___ ___ ___

___ ___ ___ ___

Expiry date _____ Signature _____

Fax this form to Currency House Inc. at: 02 9319 3649

Or post to: Currency House Inc., PO Box 2270, Strawberry Hills NSW 2012 Australia

CURRENCY HOUSE